LIGHT *and* GLORIE

Edited by Aidan Coleman & Thom Sullivan

pantaenuspress

Pantaenus Press
508 High Street
Preston Vic. 3072
Australia

Pantaenus Press is an imprint of Mosaic Resources Pty Ltd

ISBN 9781743240953

First published 2012

Cataloguing-in-Publication entry is available for the National Library of Australia http:/catalogue.nla.gov.au/.

Photography by Thom Sullivan
Printed by Openbook Howden

We would like to acknowledge the Red Room Company for a generous contribution to the cost of producing the book. We would also like to acknowledge Mark Worthing at Pantaenus Press, and Hugh McGinlay at Mosaic Resources for seeing merit in the project. Finally, we would like to thank the St. Bart's congregation for their generosity, particularly the Minister, John Miller, Julie and Alan Adcock, Mark Keough and those who assisted in running the November 10th reading.

The Windows

Lord, how can man preach thy eternall word?
    He is a brittle crazie glasse:
Yet in thy temple thou dost him afford
    This glorious and transcendent place,
    To be a window, through thy grace.

But when thou dost anneal in glasse thy storie,
    Making thy life to shine within
The holy Preachers, then the light and glorie
    More rev'rend grows, and more doth win;
    Which else shows watrish, bleak, and thin.

Doctrine and life, colours and light, in one
    When they combine and mingle, bring
A strong regard and aw: but speech alone
    Doth vanish like a flaring thing,
    And in the eare, not conscience ring.

GEORGE HERBERT (1593–1633)

CONTENTS

In 2011 I was commissioned by the Red Room Company to write a poem or poems about my experience of a club or society. I chose St. Bart's Anglican Church in Norwood because, besides loving the people whom I have come to know over the past seven years, I have always admired the church's windows. St. Bart's is one of Adelaide's oldest churches and its stained glass includes two Art Deco windows, designed by Melbourne artist Napier Waller, one of which appeared on a Christmas stamp in the 1980s.

There are many poems about works of art (ekphrastic poems you might call them) but in a long literary tradition I couldn't think of any poem about stained glass since George Herbert wrote *The Windows* in the 1630s.

I began the project by inviting the poet Thom Sullivan to write with me and take photos. We brought a pile of books along and enjoyed some idle and digressive afternoons. It occurred to us that this would be a good exercise for other poets too: the brilliance of the windows, the church's sometimes-quiet, and the challenge of a writing assignment.

Some thirty poets took up this challenge and most produced more than one poem; in some cases: four, five or six. Those who came at busy times found something akin to the buzz of a shopfloor with clicking cameras, literary gossip, the scratching of pens and the soft rain of type; at other times – slightly awkward – maybe us and one other poet.

But the poets came and they wrote. We began with the idea of an evening reading alongside backlit stained glass and thought to perhaps produce a short chapbook. But we soon realised that such a meagre publication would not do the poems justice. And so this book, *Light & Glorie*, its title (and spelling) honouring Herbert's poem.

The book features many of South Australia's – and Australia's – finest poets, showcasing a broad array of styles, with each poet bringing their particular style and idiosyncrasies. Their responses range from devotional to sceptical, from detailed to digressive from the personal and aesthetic to the historical. All the material in this book is new work, generated by the poets' responses to the windows.

W.H. Auden thought art the chief means of 'breaking bread with the dead'; these poems write back to the windows, their creators and sponsors, and the past lives re-imagined. More importantly they break bread with the living: rendering the strange, familiar and eloquent; the familiar, eloquent and strange.

AIDAN COLEMAN, OCTOBER 2012

St. Bart's Windows

Its blazoned characters are like Tarot cards.
The necessary knight, St. George,
Is armoured in faith's finery,
Gazing blankly, bored as a rock star
Dazed by another camera flash.
St. Alban in bright fancy dress, a Roman soldier's garb,
Is haughty as a fashion model stalled on a runway.
The pair of Christs are wraithlike, tired.
One's a wan Light of the World,
Lost and uncertain, with lamp in hand;
The other's looking skyward from the cross
His mind on going home.

Best is the nativity in open air,
Mary with Baby J. in arms.
He wears a lifebuoy halo of red and white,
And she a round and luminous disk,
Like a hat for going to the races.
Her face has a childcare worker's patience,
But at her bare feet is a stream with two arched fish
That seem in pain. This small detail,
Marginalia on an illustrated manuscript,
Offers the rawest feeling.
I want to ask why it hurts them so.
A foreseen grief?
Mary knows and does not need to tell.

St. Bartholomew's Church, Norwood

On entering St. Bartholomew's Church, I am washed
with a gentle calm akin to slow rivers and soft leaves.
Stained-glass windows, like keyholes to heaven bring
blessings of light from above. Even a cobweb swings
serenely, in time to a high draft, tickling young John's ear
as he stands beside Jesus and the bearded apostles.

The wooden ceiling is like the hull of an upturned boat.
In rows of red-cushioned pews its crew gathers
and sings, sailing to salvation under the guidance
and illumined eyes of Christ and the saints.
In the foyer, the Mary Magdalene charity box
overflows with groceries, the urn is always bubbling
and there are welcoming smiles for all who enter.
Outside, the steep roof pushes through
white-capped sky, launching pigeons and prayers.

East Window

Out of Cappadocia he is come:
Saint George in sky-blue armour at first light,
hallowed by cold steel and the dripping blood
of the necessary dragon underfoot –

our psychic ancestor by all the signs,
roiling in agony, casting a baleful eye
back over his ransacked hoard of centuries.
Sometimes more than a scapegoat has to die

so Heaton, Butler & Bayne designed of him
a doughty container for the thing contained,
dark matter to our universe of stars,
guarding a treasure he cannot understand.

And what a piece of work! Peacock-bright,
lonely as the underside of a stone,
seductive as the shining Prince of Darkness,
innocent as a lizard in the sun,

and immaculate in his viridescent scales,
those diminuendos of lashing pain.
The beast had Buckley's chance, cursed with our sins:
treachery, avarice, cunning and disdain.

Still he guards the hinterland we are,
breathing through the shadows of our art
ambivalence and irony, the ruthless
will to prevail that served us from the start.

So here's a prayer for the paradox of Draco,
slain and resurrected in the mind;
the old saint-maker lurks in each of us.
May we not live to see his hour come round.

Fire of Faith Burning

Calm and undaunted in this place I sit.
No haunted darkness, peaceful softly lit
by the silent and searching sunlight
all life upon earth can wake
from my deadly suffering can take
bright, dazzling shadows from the night.

These window stories made from coloured pane
rainbow threading through apse and sacred lane
a child-like security re-ignites
that fire of faith burning in darkest nights
St. George's heroic inspiration
Dragon slayer's triumphal elation.

All evil mastered by the brave and good
the simple message clearly understood
A metaphor of battle we must face
to strengthen conviction and courage brace
to fight that call to selfish, cruel action
unkind, careless cold and gutted of love
Instead, reach beyond, to reach far above.

To a power sending light through the glass
sand to infinity, each grain shall pass.
The glittering white in that shaft of light
Dispelling all shadows and fears from night
Peaceful and watchful of sunbeams at play
Calm and undaunted in this place I stay.

St. George

St. George,
was he a saint?
Among dragon kind
we called him
Slayer
But who would listen
to us, figments
of the imagination
breathing fire,
tearing and rending
In reality
most of us were gentle
soft creatures
that lolled in warm shallows,
dined on seaweed
Some of us grew horny plates
for our own defence.
It is true
some of our kind
preyed on others,
but with discrimination;
they were not
reckless killers
Then came the great cataclysm,
fire over fire, thunder
and the deep roaring night.
Only our small winged kin
found food to survive
What poor dragon

did St. George prick
with his bitter blade?
Some lonely creature
long hidden, that stumbled
from a cave at dusk
and frightened by a human,
roared, the sun behind its head
mistaken for flame?
According to legend
St. George stabbed
the last of us to extinction

Or did he fight
those other monsters
that lay hidden:
pride and anger
greed and lust?
Then laid down his sword
and from the wilderness
emerged
a virtuous human.

Saint George

Saint George is frozen in glass,
spear in hand, he's eternally kept
from slaying his foe; can't even
fight off spiders and crows.

Wire mesh outside defends him
the congregation do so from within;
fire's breath, ironically, his only
threat. May Saint Florian protect.

St. George – Heaton, Butler & Bayne

St. Alban – Heaton, Butler & Bayne

St. Alban's Mother Speaks

Here he is, our boy, in his favourite shin plates.
Beaten copper they were, each one
topped with the likeness of a lion –
to ward off the enemy he said, but in truth
he liked a bit of flair and flounce.

It took me an age to embroider the hem of his tunic
the way he wanted, and then his father came home
with the cloak you see him wearing. Beautiful though it is,
no depiction could do justice to the full circle
of its sweep: a matador could fend off a bull

as quick as prick it full of sticks if he had a cloak
like that. The brooch you see at the shoulder
is a family heirloom. We'd sooner have bequeathed it
to his bride, but when it came clear there'd never be a bride,
well – he'd always admired it and wished it for his own.

And to think all of it went to adorn an impoverished priest
making his escape from soldiers, while our dear boy
went to a martyr's death in the priest's garb of drabbest brown.
Brown: he'd have hated that – not that we begrudge
the priest of course, a man of God after all.

But if any of you should discover
a pair of copper shin plates, each topped
with the head of a lion – there couldn't be but one pair
of their like – perhaps you'll return them to us.
Thank you.

In the Absence of Saints

Alban, the Cephalophore, halides

We search the periodic table of light
for the colour of your halo, the holy
translucence you must carry by hand:
perhaps the yellow of afterstorm,
so astringent as to dissolve the misted
panes that shelter us from inundation;
or green more pale than imagination,
more acrid than the anger of your prosecution,
more keen than your executioner's blade;
maybe russet, like leaves floating in couplets
on the river you hold divided, the whirlpools
and eddies you piously, endlessly, still.
What chance, then, of violet, with the lustre
of precious metal, smelted from mouldering
sea-wrack, the stink of belated landfall?
Fluorine, chlorine, bromine, iodine:
salts of treasured earth, elementary vapours
dissipating with death's eye departed.

George, the Dragon slayer, oxides

Red iron, clay, parareptilian exhalation,
horizon, horizons east and west, plumes
armoured for battle, declarations of war,
the wheel of lacerating swords, disbelief,
rotation from one life to another, a cross.
White tin, sand untrammelled, parchment

primed for translation into otherworldliness,
lunar crescent rising, falling, three breaths
framed, waves receding like a princess, veiled,
this swoon of uncertainty before illumination.

Bartholomew, Nathaniel, crystalline

Streaming from galaxies
more distant than angels,
the incandescence of creation,
the fluctuating luminosity
that brings sanctity of relief
to your bloody flay,
that carries you here
across anonymous oceans,
all weight of evidence
secure within your ark,
your testimony revealed
by lead and stain and glass.

Virgin and Child

in a certain light her smile –
if it is a smile – is all eyes

& almost flirtatious, defiant
offering something complex

that might trouble us
if we try to define it

she meets our gaze or gazes
beyond us, knowable

& yet remote from us
her gesture refers us to the child

who simply defers us back
her gaze, her gesture, his gaze

& night over the sleeping city
& the star shrill as ice.

That Other Star

It would happen
on a purple night, the darkness
pierced by a star ever so
marginally brighter to those who knew
what to look for. Mary holds
Christ's attentive weight – God
struck wordless by a mother's love –
and the townsfolk gather

as at a doorway –
in Mary's blue radiance – impatient
for immanence,
each unaware
of that other star, not silver
but a diamond of blood.

Under the Nativity

Underneath her sandalled feet
steps marble down
to the river
where a fish rises up
out of the watery pane –
mouth agape, teeth bared,
its fishy-eye convex,
emptied of any thought
save the vision
up and out of the water
gasping in the air
glassy gasping for the view –
bearing aqueous witness
swimming up
out of its own life
its own stream of consciousness
into our life here
forever hereafter.

Nativity – Napier Waller (1938)

Nativity

This dragonfly-wing holds the nave aloft
crystalline star fracturing heaven's end
motherhood honoured in the shallows.
They assemble, night-soaked
Bethlehem stacked purple at their backs
gazing out steadily, no joy or tears,
indifferent to the paradox
of needing day to light this endless night.
Only the child twists for air
cracking the watery surface
his scarlet halo leaping from the frame
the vivid shade of immanence, memory
and the odd, portentous star.

The Other Blue Woman

the other blue woman
is very different to me
seated with a child on her lap
hair cut short – face angular
an almost masculine beauty
angelic yet so ordinary
serene solemn sombre
eyes convey such sadness
weariness

husband stands behind
beyond him another family
the mother holds a lamb
fish – leap at the feet
of this other blue woman
inscription reads "to the memory of
Charlotte Elizabeth Wall
a mother beloved
a gift from her family"
a mother unlike me
who has never had children
of her own only three sons
on borrowed time

West Window

This woman with a baby on her lap,
upright as an iris stem,
one bloom, one bud,
holds in her poise all women
cradling the light of the world
in Syria, Sudan, Nineveh, Memphis, Ur.
And the one I sat with for an hour,
Thursday, the week of the bus strike,
in a racketty second-class train carriage,
the nine am to town,
a plain woman smiling the wider
for a hare lip and the joy of
taking the baby on her lap,
Vietnamese, with a matching smile,
in for the surgery she herself never had.
I'm thinking of that woman with her child,
nervous, happy, leaning a little
forward as she spoke, beatific
in a sort of suburban way
being blessed for a moment
with the clarity of glass, a window, say,
through which I might have caught
a glimpse of the Nativity,
this window by which I now remember her.

All Births are Precious Gifts

Infant child born in stable innocent
a blessed birth by herald angels' call
Yet, in his crib, he looks not heaven sent
too small and pure to suffer for us all.

All births are precious gifts of love and life
each child to each parent a sweet delight
harmony's bond between husband and wife
glittering hope for a future made bright.

Tender shoot we nurture and grow
tall and strong to adult flower
watched each day and passing hour
from the first day the seed was sown.

This baby born to cradle misery
to promise man eternity
must give his life to settle sin
and hold the pain of love within.

Infant child whose birth-story told in glass
a blessed life through light shall pass
Yet, in his crib so seeming meek and mild
this perfect hope, this perfect child.

Shine you bright stars, fling your light spears
Pierce sharp the heart of all our fears
Reach beyond all time and space
to look upon that Holy face.

Somewhere in our dreams and imagining
locked in patterns bold and captivating.
Release us now to simple golden days
dancing along light's shaft where colours play

with blues of the sky, the river and sea
unfettered beauty rich, vibrant and free
leaping with life-energy from the sun
until our long days are over and done.

The Light of the World

He is robed and carrying a lantern,
bloodless crown of thorns
under a royal circlet.
Can such a dim lamp illumine the whole world?

It seems like a candle,
like the kindly light that leads
amidst the encircling gloom.

But the true light
hides behind the sunlight
the dark and the night stars,
is not formed from photons,
lives within us,
shines out, surprising in the darkest places.

King of Kings

Obsequious sycophants
Exalt Him.
Elevate Him.

Distance him.

O Lord
O Majesty
O great and good, so far above us
We are not worthy.

He comes knocking
But we
wretched sinners
do we answer the call?
We are less than weeds at his feet.

Except that's not right.
Christ was never above humanity.
In this window
The man I know
has, like that other king,
left the building.

The Light of the World

after William Holman Hunt

*Behold, I stand at the door and knock; if any man hear My voice, and open
the door, I will come in to him, and will sup with him, and he with Me.*
Revelation 3:20

I supped with him long ago
Laughing, free from care
Wine was drunk, bread broken
Stories told & retold
They were good days sure
But as mortal things go
Time & doubt drew us apart
Our friendship rankled grew
I lived alone, overgrown
For a score of years
Till he came again, knocked
Upon my handle-less door
At first I did not notice
Then did not know how
But softly knock he ever did
Till
Somewhere deep I heard it
Somewhere deep I knew
& all was as it ever was
But better now because true

The days of heaven are never numbered
No matter how many mockingbirds are killed

Light of the World – H.L. Vosz

St. John the Evangelist (from the *North Window*) – W. Waites (1872)

The North Windows

In a miracle of stained glass,
John the Apostle, his face aglow,
stands beside his cousin, Jesus.
The other apostles, gathered here also,
are hirsute with the years of their wisdom.
But John, the boy apostle, is smooth of skin.
Not even the beginnings of a beard
stubble the glass.

One day, for his devotion,
he will be plunged in boiling oil,
and all those present, seeing him emerge unscathed,
will join him in praise of God's grace
just as you see him here,
the sanguineous red of his coat,
and his rapture at the risen Christ,
dripping light.

On the Transportation of the North Window

Dismantle the beards and the odd feet,
the green of date palms and paned faces,
the urgent sky's banner
and dinner plate haloes;

fracture with care
the bended knees, the fingers pointing
to already over.

Dis-piece the wing-stumps
of angels' shoulders,
blunt Christ's aphorisms: word by word;

flat-pack and taxi through electric dusk,
to rise again in the East.

Medea's Salvation

– inspired by the Altar Window

Trace my body with a blade on glass cut from Colchis
edge of this earth, years away from Adelaide.
Colour me golden, purple and red and let there be
smoothed flame surrounding my head; hang me a small banner
for I so loveth man and please place my two boys please
as angels in each of my two hands. Then begin: the organ, the candles
fill all of these pews – someone stand up to sing me the news.

Where is God in this city of churches?
*Fleeing from newborn to newest
in the Women's and Children's Hospital.*
And Hecate, where is she?
Clothed in the gear of a Rundle Mall busker.
What about forgiveness for our memories?
*Not in the scuffed soles of the black-footed
walking in front of Parliament House.*

I am powerless watching my bus drive off, looking out
not beyond; a magpie shits on my shoulder and then flies north
*and prayer is the span of the magpie's wings
in its lifting from this earthbound world.*

Stained Glass Windows

At St. Cyprian's child me watches sun through a stained glass window
Time hangs like a bat entombed
As the priest intones the long service
Three women at the empty tomb
And the light leads me on
In London in some provincial church I watch sun through a window
St. Paul on his horse blinded by Christ
And that same sun later rests on a lone coffin there
And the light deepens
And now at St. Barts I watch again sun through stained glass
Christ instructing the eleven disciples
Jig sawed glass in red blue green and gold
And the light steadies me on.

The Sadness of Stained Glass Faces

Step through the gates off Beulah Road
another world, not Norwood,
quaint reminder of a time forgot.
Anglican Church of Australia reads Oz
but Holman Hunt's *The Light of the World*
could easily come with his lantern
knocking at this door to light
the mother's hallowed anguish
the soldier with the piercing spear
St. Alban beheaded for his faith
St. George the Christian Roman soldier
put to death for his belief.

These windows are emotion filled
and you are drawn to witness, mark
the sadness of these stained glass faces
from a time so long ago
yet here around you still.
Look closely at the faces of St. Bart's.
for others also shine, and these
not etched with sadness or distress.
Jesus with disciples, talks
a mother's love of newborn babe
and winged angels carolling:
Lovest thou ME and *Feed MY Sheep.*
A dove proclaiming gently:
In this cross, Salvation.

What past and present link
do all these faces have in common?
Below the faces are the names

once members living
now etched with loving care
the Hunts, the Andrews, Walls
the Gosses (explorer, soldier, father, son)
and others gone before.
Thus in one stroke revealed
connection with the name cards in the Nave…
Alcock, Coleman, Derwick, Pengelly
and congregation present.
A timeless faith links stained glass faces
and St. Bart's at 10, today
a simple clear relation.
Decide to enter through this door
and you will find: *Salvation.*

Calvary

Almost out of sight and mind
a tragedy is quietly being recounted
in the pellucid story
of this chancel window.
Intimate as an x ray,
the muted light diagnoses
the crux of Christ's pain
as he suffers the torture
of metal driven through bone
while his mother looks on
as helpless as the mother
who waits by her son,
broken and bleeding
from the speeding car;
his limbs fixed to the frame
on the hospital bed:
metal rods in his feet,
halo traction in his head.

JOHN PFITZNER

Crucifixion

Don't read this image literally.
Crucifixion was never so clean,
the nailed body so graceful.
The agony here is in the faces
of the faithful, not the victim,
whose arms are raised as if in victory,
his eyes as if in quiet triumph.

The language here is that of parable,
history translated into metaphor:
the redemptive power
in a martyr's death;
the beauty of a truthful life;
and in a world where people suffer,
the possibility of grace.

Crucifixion – Napier Waller (1941)

Of Pieces of Glass and the Broken Christ

The wounded one
betrayed
broken
suspended between heaven and earth
within the abyss
The city behind him
rising from the ground as earth coloured blocks and
dissolving upward into streaks of colour
Like rain down glass

I imagine the fragments
The story broken into pieces
Nothing more than shapes of glass
and dull lead outlines
malleable, warpable, poisonous

And I think of the suffering
locked within our wounded
Misshapen fragments
untold stories
poisonous, broken, frameworks

And long for the craftsmen
to lay the pieces on the table
to mould the framework
into a whole
and gently lay in the pieces

So that the stories become whole
That the light may illuminate
and that passersby will look on
and marvel
and be enriched.

In Hac (Cruce) Salus

in this (cross) salvation

The Greek word ΙΗΣΟΥΣ,
Jesus
The Latin **IHS** *Iesus Hominum Salvator*
      Jesus, Saviour of Men

In the Nicene Creed – *Symbolum Nicaenum*
Jesus was conceived by
The Holy Spirit
THE DOVE
The giver of life
    as
WIND
LIGHT
OIL   and
FIRE

Pneumatology* traces the lead of
the stained glass regal stance and colours
befit for the King of Kings
through *Hermes Trismegistus*
Divine source of Wisdom   as
Greek Hermes and Egyptian Thoth
gods of writing, magic and wisdom
guides of souls to the afterlife
        foretold
Corpus Christi a priori *Corpus hermeticum*
due to the thrice wise *Trismegistus*

who foresaw the coming of Christ*

Jesus came to cast fire on the earth (LK 12:40)
      FIRE
The transforming energy of the Spirit
    For God is a spirit (John 4:24)

And according to John
No man has seen God at any time

My head bowed

In Hac Salus
returns me to Grecian Hornopoles*

    –   theology of holy spirit
    –   found in writings of Augustine, Giordano Bruno, Campanella
    –   cult centre of Thoth/Hermes: gods of magic, healing, wisdom
         and the patrons of scribes

Stained-glass Redemption

In your stains of sin and grace
see my colours, shapes;
we have our filters
you and I.
Like the artisan
who worked my pigments and dyes
hammered outlines
and soldered joints
you forge your own beliefs
you construct truths
and cast judgements.
In the morning
incident light through me
is luminous with promise,
in the evening
diffused, reflective,
like later in your life.
We endure through the ages,
you and I,
remarkable, fragile,
each testament to an artist's vision.
I am eyes to your soul.

Church Music

1. Chorus

We are drab and glorious,
Plain and beautiful as air,
Outside's blue kerosene vapour
Breathes through us all day.

We're cardboard cut-outs
Living on borrowed light,
Frozen medieval glossies,
The slowest of slide shows.

We may be ghosts
But we know desire.
When you look away from us
We still flicker in the corner of your eye.

2. Solo

By day I am all Disney,
Gaudy as Gaudi in my glassy gladrags,
A vivid test pattern portrait.

At dusk the light begins creeping back out
Through my brittle skin
To the speckled sky.

Nights it's like sleep.
Days it's like dreaming.
There's no stiller life than mine.

Red Room Church, Holy Saturday 2012

I take a photo of the crucifixion
in stained glass; and it goes black
and says "Change the battery pack"

While other poets are busy snapping away
North, South, East and West, laying
groundwork for ekphrastic homework

It looks like I'm stuck with memory again
Looking askance through panes of imagination
or some theological caution

A bit like Dickinson's slant of light, and
Heft of cathedral tunes, or MacDiarmid's
innumerable Christs dying under skies like pitch

Speaking of which, I'm sure
I said "bugger" when the camera failed just now
risking my soul

Audibly, under an Anglican apse
Possessed by the script
from an old Hugh Grant movie

Faith, Likened to Stained Glass

I have lingered here long enough
admiring this varicoloured glass,

to learn the paradox of the window's stasis
and the light's constant flux; the polychrome tints

feinting when the sun
is sealed off by a veil of cloud

or revived when the veil lifts
and the light rushes through.

The Benediction of Sunlight

Wiped feet, but still the world
is dragged in on my polluted soles.
The nave's air clasps above me in prayer,
gaze averted with almost papal decorum.

The hushed rustle, creak of knees and pew,
the points of ache where body meets wood
and I am back in childhood like a prayer-book
falling open to the needed page.

Decades on and the words rise,
body and throat falling into the rhythms
as if waiting, stored in my cells,
tiny monks in silent seclusion.

Back then I walked away, shackles of fact
worn jauntily like silver anklets.
And although it is easily said – God is love –
hypocrisy cannot be so simply forgiven.

The windows, jewelled arrow slits
filter away earthly distractions leaving only
the call and response, hymn and psalm,
the benediction of the sun.

Dust motes glow, their gilded swing
falling softly like forgiveness.
I bend my head, hoping to catch
their gentle blessing.

But I don't feel it.
I don't feel it.

Outside, face lifted to the light
slicing down through the glorious world
it is this, this embedded divinity,
this is all I ask of a God.

My Side of the Window

We enter small
like mice through the cracks of the church door.
In my hand, my daughter's hand.
I follow where she goes.

Between us, the light dust. Icons gleam.
I face the saint on the glass window.
My side of the glass window.

The faith in me celebrates Him
lifted up
where the Sun rises with wings
and swards shimmer with sharpness.

For him, our family's Bread
cross cut, kissed and turned around
with hands passed on from father to son.

With the Sun,
a mother and a daughter
approaching slowly
peek through the stained glass window
remembering to fear.
To kneel, kiss and pray?

Instead
I search for words to describe and define
the circle of life and the power of something.

My angel asks:
'Who is our patron?'
'Someone who looks after our family,
watches over you.'
'*You,* Mum.'

My wings grow.
I kneel to her, I kiss her. I shine.
I carry my arms like a sword and a shield.

Behind the sunlight sharpness
I pray to be an icon in her eyes
just a little bit longer.

Hymn

Listen with your eyes; I have a silence to sing you: *the human body is ninety-nine percent light.*

Can't you feel the photons passing through dark stroma to the breathless lumen at your core? Can't you feel your atoms unravelling in light as it travels your arterial pathways? Can't you feel it spiralling round the bronchioli's broccoli, mushrooming in your myocardium?

Not the thick orange light of the pungent sun but the pure white light of more distant stars. Not a bright new light but a light that aches with age, its droplets caught in the web of your bones.

It is pinging at your heartstrings, singing from your fingertips, springing from your shoulders in iridescent wings.

You catch a hand to your mouth to contain it but even the rain cannot hold so much light. Not the rain. Not even the sky.

Light & Glorie is a wonderful collection of poetry inspired by the beauty of the stained glass of St. Bart's Anglican Church in Norwood, South Australia. Reading the poems brought to mind two thoughts, one poetic and the other about the especial beauty that stained glass can convey. William Wordsworth wrote of "Thoughts that do often lie too deep for tears" while a distant relative of mine, Hugh Arnold (author of *Stained Glass of the Middle Ages in England and France*) described stained glass through "that dazzling and glowing labyrinth of coloured jewels a past age is speaking far more articulately, if one stops to unravel the message, than ever in stone or wood".

Reading this collection of poems, I encountered deep thoughts evoked by the "glowing labyrinth of coloured jewels" that are the stained glass windows of St. Bart's. In the diverse approaches of the poets, we find ourselves at times moved profoundly, at others challenged philosophically, even theologically, while at others a wry smile forms on our lips.

Unfair though it is to quote from only a handful of this excellent selection of thirty-four poems, I feel the need to give some quotes to be ambassadors for all the poems in explanation of my description of the anthology's diversity. Take St. George, for example, variously referred to as "the necessary knight", "that fire of faith burning in darkest nights", through to a dragon's point of view of him as "slayer ... with his bitter blade" or a "frozen in glass" saint unable to "fight off spiders and crows".

Then we have the poets describe the living entity that stained glass becomes in the ever-changing light that shines through it. A living sight to match the theology of the living word that depicts an "embedded divinity" from "the story broken into pieces / nothing more than shapes of glass" that convey "through the sadness of these stained glass faces" that "fracture with care / the bended knees, the fingers pointing" to what "might trouble us / if we try to define it" "so that the stories become whole / that the light may illuminate".

John Riches writes of how poetry can be "an exploration of the creative power and the glory of God" and quotes Gerard Manley Hopkins:

"Glory be to God for dappled things …"

The dappled images of the stained glass of St. Bart's, Norwood, has inspired this wonderful collection of poetry whose creative power moves us and glorifies God. My congratulations to all involved in this wonderful project.

DR LYNN ARNOLD AO

JUDE AQUILINA publishes poetry, short fiction and nonfiction. She lives in the Adelaide Hills and is a freelance writer, editor, mentor and workshop leader. She teaches in the Professional Writing Unit at Adelaide College of the Arts.

LYNETTE ARDEN'S first collection of poetry *A Pause in the Conversation* was published in *New Poets 15*.

ANN BARSON has worked as a teacher, actor and puppeteer. She acted for the BBC Radio for thirteen years, and also wrote a play on her childhood for them.

MARTIN CHRISTMAS is a professional theatre director, teacher and playwright. In 2012 he has been a Friendly Street mentored poet. He is published in *Redoubt* (University of Canberra) and Friendly Street Poets 36.

AIDAN COLEMAN divides his working life between teaching and speechwriting. His second book of poetry is *Asymmetry* (Brandl & Schlesinger, 2012).

KATE DELLER-EVANS' teaches at Flinders University and in her PhD researched verse novels for children and young adults, including writing one called *Copper Coast*. She was also a Friendly Street *New Poet 7*.

JELENA DINIC came to Australia in 1993 and later completed a BA at the University of SA. She writes in Serbian and in English and her work has appeared in readers, journals and websites.

M.L. EMMETT is from Reading (UK), and works as an editor, writer, reviewer and poet. She is a past Convenor of Friendly Street Poets, and the Director of Poetry and Art Oz. poetryandartoz@gmail.com

STEVE EVANS teaches writing at Flinders University. He is the author/editor of 11 books, including six of his poetry. His prizes include the Queensland Premier's Poetry Award and a Barbara Hanrahan Fellowship.

MARGARET FENSOM has published poems and short stories in journals and anthologies and is part author of Friendly Street *New Poets 12*. She studies theology part time at St. Barnabas' College.

Originally from Scotland, ALISON FLETT has been living in Adelaide for the past two years. Her book of poetry *Whit Lassyz Ur Inty* was published by Argyll Press (2004) and was shortlisted for the Saltire Book of the Year Award.

IAN GIBBINS is a neuroscientist and Professor of Anatomy at Flinders University. His poems have also been published in Canada and France. His first full collection *Urban Biology* with accompanying CD was published in 2012.

HEATHER TAYLOR JOHNSON is a poetry editor for *Wet Ink* and the author of two books. Her third book of poetry (IP Press) and her first novel (HarperCollins) will be released in 2013.

GARETH RIO JONES' first collection was published in Friendly Street's *New Poets 17* (2012). He believes any place which helps you see the gods is a temple.

JENNIFER LISTON is the author of three poetry collections. She has a degree in electronic engineering from the University of Limerick and a Master of Arts in Creative Writing from the University of Adelaide. http://jenniferliston.com

LOUISE MCKENNA was born in the United Kingdom. Her first poetry collection was *A Lesson in Being Mortal* (Wakefield Press 2010). She is co editor of *Flying Kites,* Friendly Street Reader 36, (2012).

RACHAEL MEAD was published in Friendly Street's *New Poets 17* (2012) and she was shortlisted in the 2012 Adelaide Festival Literature Awards for an unpublished manuscript.

DAVID MORTIMER writes poems to read aloud. His third collection, *Magic Logic* (Puncher & Wattmann, 2012) includes poems shortlisted for the Blake, Newcastle, and Montreal poetry prizes.

LOUISE NICHOLAS has been publishing poetry for over 15 years. The highlights of a recent trip overseas included attending a poetry workshop in Maine (USA) and several meetings of the Pitshanger Poets in Ealing, London.

JAN OWEN'S most recent book is *Poems 1980–2008*. A selection in Dutch, *Der Kus,* was published in 2010, and a New and Selected, *The Offhand Angel*, is forthcoming in the UK with Eyewear Publishing.

JOHN PFITZNER'S first collection, *Fence Music*, was published in Friendly Street's *New Poets 17* (2012). He has co-edited three poetry anthologies, including *Metabolism*. Before retirement he worked as a publishing house editor.

SUZANNE REECE has worked as a teacher, and small business owner, and is now training in radio. Her life is scattered on myriad pieces of paper, and she is still hopeful of getting them under control someday.

LIDIJA ŠIMKUTĖ writes in Lithuanian and English. Her poetry is translated into fifteen languages and she has translated Australian literature and other works into Lithuanian. www.ace.net.au/lidija

THOM SULLIVAN is a poet, editor and photographer. His first collection of poems, *Airborne*, was published in Friendly Street's *New Poets 14* (2008).

RUSS TALBOT has degrees in computing, management and communication, and is currently studying Professional Writing at ACArts in this one. He is interested in just about everything – even things that don't interest him.

G.M. WALKER is a local Adelaide poet and spoken word performer. Her collection of poems: "blue woman"(BookEnds, 2006) sadly sold out.